MW01290771

I think the series is wonderful and beneficial for tourists to get information before visiting the city.

-Seckin Zumbul, Izmir Turkey

I am a world traveler who has read many trip guides but this one really made a difference for me. I would call it a heartfelt creation of a local guide expert instead of just a guide.

-Susy, Isla Holbox, Mexico

New to the area like me, this is a must have!

-Joe, Bloomington, USA

This is a good series that gets down to it when looking for things to do at your destination without having to read a novel for just a few ideas.

-Rachel, Monterey, USA

Good information to have to plan my trip to this destination.

-Pennie Farrell, Mexico

Aptly titled, you won't just be a tourist after reading this book. You'll be greater than a tourist!

-Alan Warner, Grand Rapids, USA

Thank you for a fantastic book.

-Don, Philadelphia, USA

BRZENK

Great ideas for a port day.

-Mary Martin USA

Even though I only have three days to spend in San Miguel in an upcoming visit, I will use the author's suggestions to guide some of my time there. An easy read - with chapters named to guide me in directions I want to go.

-Robert Catapano, USA

Great insights from a local perspective! Useful information and a very good value!

-Sarah, USA

This series provides an in-depth experience through the eyes of a local. Reading these series will help you to travel the city in with confidence and it'll make your journey a unique one.

-Andrew Teoh, Ipoh, Malaysia

Tourists can get an amazing "insider scoop" about a lot of places from all over the world. While reading, you can feel how much love the writer put in it.

-Vanja Živković, Sremski Karlovci, Serbia

GREATER THAN A TOURIST – PLACE CHIANG MAI THAILAND

50 Travel Tips from a Local

Mandy Brzenk

BRZENK

Cover designed by

Greater Than a Tourist

Visit our website at www.GreaterThanaTourist.com

Lock Haven, PA

ISBN: 9781976769580

>TOURIST

50 TRAVEL TIPS FROM A LOCAL

BRZENK

BOOK DESCRIPTION

Are you excited about planning your next trip?

Do you want to try something new?

Would you like some guidance from a local?

If you answered yes to any of these questions, then this Greater Than a Tourist book is for you.

Greater Than a Tourist – Chiang Mai, Thailand by Mandy Brzenk offers the inside scoop on Chiang Mai. Most travel books tell you how to travel like a tourist. Although there is nothing wrong with that, as part of the Greater Than a Tourist series, this book will give you travel tips from someone who has lived at your next travel destination.

In these pages, you will discover advice that will help you throughout your stay. This book will not tell you exact addresses or store hours but instead will give you excitement and knowledge from a local that you may not find in other smaller print travel books.

Travel like a local. Slow down, stay in one place, and get to know the people and the culture. By the time you finish this book, you will be eager and prepared to travel to your next destination.

BRZENK

TABLE OF CONTENTS

13. Ride In A Tuk-tuk, But Maybe Just Once

14. Know About Upcoming Buddhist Holidays

15. Take A Songtaew

16. Enjoy Nightlife Before Midnight

17. Seek Out The Good Coffee

18. Let The Seasons Help You Decide Your Travel Dates

19. Take "Impossible" Photos At Art In Paradise

20. Visit The Royal Botanical Gardens

21. Bargain For Souvenirs At the Night Bazaar And Then Eat At The Food Court

22. Don't Let The Bugs And Lizards Bother You

23. Check Out The Many Vegetarian- and Vegan-Friendly Restaurants

24. Know The Bathroom 411

25. Try The Fresh Fruit

26. Watch A Muay Thai Fight, Or Take A Class!

27. Plan A Day Trip To Doi Inthanon

28. Eat Thai Curry

29. Grab Dinner At One Of The Nightly Food Markets

30. Visit The Grand Canyon And Its New Water Park

31. Get Soaked During Songkran

32. Watch A Cabaret Show

33. Travel On A Budget With Ease

34. Eat At Cherng Doi Chicken

35. Take A Trip To Mon Cham

DEDICATION

This book is dedicated to Pubpup, for helping me to fall so deeply in love with Chiang Mai that I began to call it home.

BRZENK

ABOUT THE AUTHOR

Mandy Brzenk is an American From Milwaukee, Wisconsin. She traveled solo to Thailand to teach English in 2015 with plans to return home after one year. Almost 3 years later, she still lives in Chiang Mai with her partner, who she met during her first visit to the city.

Mandy loves to immerse herself in new things: cultures, fields of study, and physical activities. Her greatest interests include weight training, writing, and holistic health and wellness.

BRZENK

HOW TO USE THIS BOOK

The Greater Than a Tourist book series was written by someone who has lived in an area for over three months. The goal of this book is to help travelers either dream or experience different locations by providing opinions from a local. The author has made suggestions based on their own experiences. Please do your own research before traveling to the area in case the suggested places are unavailable.

BRZENK

FROM THE PUBLISHER

Traveling can be one of the most important parts of a person's life. The anticipation and memories that you have are some of the best. As a publisher of the Greater Than a Tourist book series, as well as the popular 50 Things to Know book series, we strive to help you learn about new places, spark your imagination, and inspire you. Wherever you are and whatever you do I wish you safe, fun, and inspiring travel.

Lisa Rusczyk Ed. D.
CZYK Publishing

BRZENK

OUR STORY

Traveling is a passion of the "Greater than a Tourist" series creator. Lisa studied abroad in college, and for their honeymoon Lisa and her husband toured Europe. During her travels to Malta, an older man tried to give her some advice based on his own experience living on the island since he was a young boy. She was not sure if she should talk to the stranger but was interested in his advice. When traveling to some places she was wary to talk to locals because she was afraid that they weren't being genuine. Through her travels, Lisa learned how much locals had to share with tourists. Lisa created the "Greater Than a Tourist" book series to help connect people with locals. A topic that locals are very passionate about sharing.

BRZENK

WELCOME TO
> TOURIST

BRZENK

INTRODUCTION

"You will never be completely at home again, because part of your heart always will be elsewhere. That is the price you pay for the richness of loving and knowing people in more than one place."

-Miriam Adeney

Travel is an opportunity to enrich our perspectives on ourselves, other people, and the world as a whole. It is this more than anything else, in my opinion. And while spending an extended amount of time in any foreign place allows for the greatest benefit, our outlooks will begin to shift immediately if we take advantage of each opportunity that any new place offers us. This requires us to step outside our comfort zones and actively try to understand the culture we find ourselves in. For this reason, it is highly encouraged for travelers to taste unusual foods, converse earnestly with locals, and appreciate—rather than simply tolerate—the unfamiliar. This book is filled with recommendations and caveats that should guide anyone visiting Chiang Mai toward an auspicious experience. Regardless of the activities you choose, if you decide to bend each travel experience into a positive one, you will inspire yourself to grow.

BRZENK

1. Get The Lay Of The Land

Chiang Mai is nestled among the mountains of Northern Thailand. Thus, it is a valley surrounded by abundant lush greenery and national parks. There are nearly 1,000,000 people within the metropolitan area of Chiang Mai, although the smaller municipal district makes up a fraction of that population. The heart of Chiang Mai is the old city. This area is a perfect square surrounded by a moat and remnants of a wall built for defense when Chiang Mai was the capital of the Lanna Kingdom more than half a century ago. It has a rich history and plenty of preserved buildings, temples, and monuments. The old city today is eccentric, very cultural and full of travelers' needs: accommodations, restaurants, tourist offices, money exchanges, coffee shops, boutiques and small stores, temples, taxis and rental shops. Another bustling area of Chiang Mai is about 2 kilometers from the old city, nicknamed "Nimman" for the main road running through the area: Nimmanahaeminda Road. Here you'll find more modern architecture, trendy cafes, galleries, tons of restaurants, Maya shopping center, and plenty of stores for shopping. In order to get a well-rounded experience of Chiang Mai, you would do well to spend some time in both of these areas as well as the mountainous outskirts.

2. Try Khao Soi

Khao soi is a famous northern Thai dish that you won't be able to find in other parts of Thailand. The broth of khao soi is curry-based with coconut milk, which is ladled on top of long egg noodles and garnished with crunchy noodles. It is normally served with pickled greens, shallots, and lime for you to add in yourself. Khao soi can be found at many Thai restaurants in the city, but the best recipes are generally found where khao soi is the specialty. Some of these places include Khao Soi Mae Sai, Khao Soi Khun Yai, and Khao Soi Chai Soi. As you can see, it's all in the name! It is worth mentioning that khao soi is mostly considered a lunchtime food, so the better places tend to stop serving it in the late afternoon. Also, this dish is often served spicy, so it may be a good idea to let staff know how spicy you would like your food to be. This advice carries over to any other Thai food you order, as well.

3. Join a Thai Cooking Class

This is a popular activity for people visiting Chiang Mai, but for good reason. Cooking classes allow you to meet new people, learn about the immense Thai food culture, and cook and eat many different foods over the course of an afternoon or evening. There are a number of cooking schools to choose from, depending on the kind of experience you want. Some schools take you to their farms outside the city and show you the inner workings of the business, and other schools take you to a nearby market to introduce you to, and purchase, the ingredients you will need for your recipes before you begin cooking. You learn quite a lot about local vegetables and herbs from these trips. During one of the classes I joined, we were even given extra time to explore the market and purchase ingredients to take home. Once you get into the kitchen, the time tends to fly as you prepare, cook, eat, and repeat until you've finished 3, 4 or 5 dishes. The instructors are experienced and knowledgeable, and they like to have fun with you during the course, so you can expect a lot of entertainment and laughter, and certainly a full belly at the end.

4. Check out Doi Suthep, Chiang Mai's Nearest Mountain

The city of Chiang Mai lies at the foot of Doi Suthep, making it a highly accessible destination. You'll find the road leading up Doi Suthep on the north-west end of the city, past Chiang Mai University and the zoo. As soon as you begin ascending the scenic mountain road, the humid air turns cool and crisp. It's a very pleasant drive with beautiful views and fresh air, and eventually, you will reach viewpoints where you can stop and admire the city below. Near the top of the mountain is the main draw for most visitors: Wat Phra That Doi Suthep, one of the most sacred temples in northern Thailand. You are welcome to respectfully explore the temple, read about its history, observe Buddhist traditions, and view Chiang Mai with a spectacular view from above. Next to the temple, you will also find food, drink, and souvenir stalls. If you continue up the mountain, you will pass by the Bhubing Palace, built for the royal family during their visits to Chiang Mai and usually open to the public. Other points of interest on Doi Suthep are numerous waterfalls, a campground, and Doi Pui Hmong Tribal Village.

5. Beware of Chiang Mai Traffic

While the region of Chiang Mai is vast, the city itself is rather small and has only a finite number of busy roads to travel by, as well as lots and lots of cars, and the longest stoplight wait times you may ever experience—it is rather common to be forced to wait at the busier traffic lights for more than 5 minutes. This combination makes for a lot of backed up traffic all around the city, especially at peak weekday times (7-9 am and 4-7 pm). This is also true during the weekend markets (see tip #9!) as you travel nearby them. For this reason, if you'll be going by way of a taxi or songtaew, or really any transportation other than motorbike or bicycle, it may take you longer than expected to reach your destination. If you will be departing during a busy hour, it would be best to leave yourself extra time.

6. Ride A Motorbike

If you have some time to practice, and/or if you feel confident driving a motorbike, it is easily the best way to get around the city. Motorbikes offer you the freedom that you don't have with taxis or songtaews, while still getting you around quicker than bicycles. Whether you're driving around the metropolitan area or exploring the lush, green city outskirts, on a motorbike, you simply get to see more! Motorbikes also make day trips to destinations outside the city a lot easier to plan, and the journey much more scenic and memorable. One of their best attributes, however, is that motorbikes can easily weave through traffic. This saves you heaps of time that you may otherwise spend in traffic jams with a hired ride. You will absolutely want to exercise caution, however. Local drivers can be unpredictable, and Thailand has a fairly high road accident rate. Because motorbikes can move faster than cars and squeeze through traffic, they can also appear out of nowhere from behind or from either side and pass by you quite closely. As crazy as it sounds, witnessing drivers turning left onto a street without so much as glancing for oncoming traffic is, in fact, a daily occurrence. It is thus important if you do feel comfortable on a motorbike, that you always wear a helmet and look in all directions before making a move.

7. Visit The Historic Temples

Chiang Mai is known for its vast number of spectacular Buddhist temples. Besides the Wat Phra That Doi Suthep, some of the most stunning wats (temples) in the city are Wat Chedi Luang, Wat Suan Dok, Wat Buppharam, and Wat Lok Moli. In reality, however, there are too many temples to name, and each building has a unique design and history. You will be sure to experience beauty, Buddhism, culture, and history at any temples you decide to visit. Some visitors like to spend a large part of a day traveling to different temples, but this could possibly be overwhelming in the heat. Another option is to intersperse temple viewings with other activities or to simply stop inside as you pass by them during your day, in order to enjoy them more fully. Unless you have a special interest in the religion or the architecture of the temples, it is likely that you will feel satisfied after visiting a few of them. However you decide to plan your visits to the temples, be sure to dress appropriately—covering your shoulders and your knees—or you will likely be asked to leave.

8. Explore Malin Market Across From Chiang Mai University

Hundreds of students and young adults, as well as families and people of all ages, visit Malin Market each evening for dinner and shopping. The market is home to a range of cuisines, from classic Thai to Japanese, burgers to barbeque, and even a new bbq-style buffet as well as snacks like ice cream, meat-on-a-stick, smoothies, fruit and waffles with toppings. Malin Market is also a fun, bustling place to shop and to check out what's trending now in Thailand. It is quite different from other markets around the city, in that it does not sell souvenirs for tourists. This market is geared toward young adult locals since it is located across the street from Chiang Mai University. So while you walk past the booths and shops, you'll find tons of clothes, shoes, accessories, electronics, and beauty products for excellent prices. It is worth noting that most often you will not be able to try on the clothes you consider purchasing, as the shops are too small for fitting rooms. If you want to be local for the evening, take a risk and buy that shirt without trying it on first! If it fits, you'll be able to show off a great memento of your visit to Chiang Mai.

9. Walk The Saturday Or Sunday Walking Street Markets

Or, like many, do both! The Saturday market and Sunday market are street markets that are closed to vehicles to make room for hundreds of people on foot. On these nights, the normally traffic-packed streets bustle instead with vendors, music, food, travelers, and locals. You can find beautiful handmade souvenirs and gifts of all kinds, support small local businesses and do some serious snacking. Many of the items for sale typify Thai culture by featuring local textiles, classic woodcraft handiwork, elephants—the national animal, and traditional dyeing techniques. You can also keep an eye out for the food stall areas and grab a seat and some street food, or choose from one of many restaurants lining the street at each market. The Saturday market takes place just outside the South gate of the old city on Wua Lai Road, while the Sunday market is nestled right in the center of the old city on Ratchadamnoen, starting at Tha Pae Gate. Both markets get going around 5:00 pm and start clearing out around 10:00 pm.

10. Take A Day Trip To The Bua Tong Sticky Waterfall

This truly unique waterfall is more than an hour outside of Chiang Mai and into the surrounding mountains, but it's well worth the trip to get there. Rent motorbikes and enjoy the beautiful scenic mountain drive, or hire a songtaew for the day! Upon arriving, you find yourself at the top of the waterfall, where there is a small shop selling grilled chicken and papaya salad, as well as a large open grassy space for picnicking and leaving your things. The waterfall itself is so extraordinary because of the type of rocks that lie underneath the rushing water. They are made of a mineral deposit that prevents algae growth, which is what would normally make them slick. Instead, the rocks feel a bit like sandpaper under your feet, and you find that you can grip them easily. With this special feature, it's possible to climb up and down the waterfall with ease! Either start at the top and climb down or walk down the stairs and work your way up the rocks, using the ropes provided if you need assistance. The sticky waterfall is a great place for travelers of all ages looking to spend time in a fun, natural setting. Bring a group and a picnic and make a day of it!

11. Go To Chinatown

One of the oldest markets in Chiang Mai is Wararot Market, also known as Chinatown. It is located just east of the old city and spans quite a large area indoors and along the street. At the many shops and stalls here, you can find all kinds of goods at basement prices. You could spend hours there, walking along the small roads and peaking into the handicraft, textile, craft supply, novelty, and clothing shops, and then wandering around inside the two indoor market spaces, where you'll find fresh and packaged foods, religious supplies, toys, housewares and much more. If the heat overwhelms you, stop at one of the street vendors for a cold juice or smoothie, a fresh coconut ready to enjoy, or other fresh fruit that can be found whole or pre-sliced for convenience. Chinatown is a great place to purchase Thai snacks to take home for yourself or others, and an even better place to experience everyday Thai culture.

12. Be Aware Of The Plastic Problem

Chiang Mai and all of Thailand is heavily reliant on the convenience of plastic. If you buy a bottle of water from a convenience store, they'll most likely put it in a bag for you, and they'll give you a plastic straw wrapped in plastic as well. Sometimes you might buy a cold drink in a plastic cup, and then they put that cup into a plastic bag for you. Sometimes you'll buy street food and they'll put it in a plastic bag, then they'll put that plastic bag into another plastic bag for carrying, plus you'll get 2 different sauces also in its own plastic bag. Along with recycling, alternatives to plastic have not quite reached the mainstream in Thailand. If you are aware of our world's plastic problem, or if you would just like to avoid a lot of extra plastic waste, you can carry your own reusable bag while out and about in Chiang Mai. It is perfectly acceptable to put your purchases in your own bag and politely refuse the plastic. Ambitious travelers can even learn to say "no bag" in Thai, which is "mai sai thung."

13. Ride In A Tuk-tuk, But Maybe Just Once

Tuk-tuks are offbeat three-wheeled rickshaw-type vehicles used as taxis throughout Thailand, and they are abundant in Chiang Mai. Tuk-tuks are a thrilling way to get around the city with the doorless, open air seating and the driver's quick weaving through traffic. They can be especially fun if you manage to find one decked out with lights and blasting music. But as exciting as they are, tuk-tuks are also one of the most expensive ways to get around Chiang Mai. Going the same distance in a songtaew or a metered taxi or an app-based ride service will be significantly cheaper. Don't miss out on a memorable experience—take a ride in a tuk-tuk while you are here! But if you're on a budget, check out the other transportation options as well.

14. Know About Upcoming Buddhist Holidays

Public holidays are plentiful in Thailand, and many of them coincide with the life and teachings of Buddha. These sacred days generally follow the moon cycle and so they will fall on different days each year. If you are in Chiang Mai on a Buddhist holiday, you will most likely find temples to be lively with ceremonies that often include candle-lit processions around the temples and meditation. Temples welcome a high volume of visitors on these sacred days, bringing offerings of candles and flowers for spirits, and food for monks. Sometimes there are city events tied with the holidays, such as performances or parades, as Thailand is a nation that loves to celebrate. You will also want to note that bars will most likely close on these holidays and you will not be able to purchase alcohol at any restaurants or shops.

15. Take A Songtaew

The most popular means of public transport for Chaing Mai locals are songtaews—red pickup trucks that have been adapted to carry passengers. They act similar to buses and therefore have lower prices than other public transport options. Like buses, songtaews normally have regular routes, but they are mostly unmarked, so you simply have to tell the driver your destination. If the driver agrees, you will want to agree on a price before hopping on. If the driver tells you no, it means he is not headed in that direction and you should flag down the next songtaew. In highly populated areas like markets and tourist destinations, songtaews are abundant, and usually, they remain parked and waiting for passengers. In other areas, you simply have to flag them down like you would a taxi. Songtaews can also be hired to drive groups to destinations outside the city. They will normally offer to drive you, wait for you at your destination, and bring you back to your accommodation for an agreed fee.

16. Enjoy Nightlife Before Midnight

Chiang Mai bars have a strictly enforced midnight closing time due to city ordinance. This also applies to stores such as 7-11, which also stop selling alcohol after midnight. Visitors are often flummoxed when the bar they've just arrived at announces last call at 11:45 pm because nightlife in other parts of Thailand will go on much later. Although the ordinance has been in place since 2014, most travelers visiting Chiang Mai learn about the midnight curfew only as the lights come on and the music stops. This is, in fact, how I personally found out about the ordinance during my first visit to Chiang Mai. Although this means that Chiang Mai is not Thailand's prime nightlife locale, you can certainly still have a fun evening at one of Chiang Mai's many unique bars. Just keep in mind, when you plan a night out in Chiang Mai, that you may want to begin your night early enough so that you can enjoy the scene while it's still buzzing. And while you are out, you can also ask some friendly locals if they know of any bars that might be disregarding the rules and staying open later.

17. Seek Out The Good Coffee

Thailand is not known for its great coffee, and, unfortunately, below-average coffee shops are around every corner. But you're in luck. There are some internationally-trained baristas scattered throughout Chiang Mai who would make any coffee connoisseur proud. Rist8o is perhaps the most popular quality spot, with a wide array of classic, signature, and even alcoholic coffee drinks served in unique glassware. Bay's Cafe—inside Food 4 Thought restaurant— also makes excellent coffee and emphasizes the brewing process. Both of these coffee shops import beans from other countries, unlike most. Fabulous Coffee is substantially less well-known, but the coffee is certainly on par and at half the price of The others. You'll find the small shop on the premises of Ramida Guesthouse near the northeast corner of the old city. The barista roasts his own coffee beans and also sells them in bulk.

18. Let The Seasons Help You Decide Your Travel Dates

The season in which you decide to visit Chiang Mai could make a world of difference for your holiday. Burning season takes place between March and May when temperatures reach 40 degrees C or 104 degrees F. This is not an ideal time to come to Chiang Mai, because on top of the extreme heat, air pollution also becomes a problem. This is, however, the season of the Thai New Year (see tip #31), which compels many to brace the weather in order to experience the exciting holiday. Next, from June to November, is rainy season. Temperatures vary during this time, but it remains hot and it also rains quite often. This weather is rather unpredictable and sudden downpours are common, but they often stop as quickly as they start. The cool season is then savored from late November to February, when temperatures are less extreme, dipping down to ~15 C or 59 F during the night. Chiang Mai sees the most visitors during this time, holds the most events, and enjoys the greatest weather.

19. Take "Impossible" Photos At Art In Paradise

Whether it's a rainy day, the heat is too sweltering, or you're just looking for some indoor fun, the 3D museum is a great option. The walls of this large museum are covered in surreal paintings that, when you stand in the right spot and have someone take your picture, magically insert you into the paintings as well! I spent an entire afternoon there during the cold season one year, and my friends and I had a fantastic time bringing the intricate murals to life. The pictures we took that day are treasures I love to revisit, and I fully intend to return when I have visitors again. Art in Paradise is a great place for all ages, so take your family or your friends. You'll have hours of fun as your camera fills up with priceless pictures of you in the ocean, above lava, hanging with pandas, and so much more.

20. Visit The Royal Botanical Gardens

Just outside the city center is Royal Flora Ratchaphruek—large botanical gardens that opened to commemorate King Bhumidol, who has since passed away, on the 60th anniversary of his reign. The vast gardens are home to thousands of species of flowers, plants, and trees over 200 acres of well-kept landscape, which you can explore on foot, bicycle, or electric tram. You will also find exhibitions showcasing different families of plant life, both indoor and outdoor, as well as beautiful artwork and architecture. The Ho Kham Royal Pavillion is perhaps the most impressive attraction of the gardens. It was designed in the style of traditional Lanna (northern Thai) architecture and features stunning craftsmanship, adornments, and artwork. I was awestruck by this pavilion during my first visit to the botanical gardens, surrounded by vivid flowers in the late-afternoon light. You'll be mesmerized by the immense beauty that these gardens hold if you decide to pay a visit.

21. Bargain For Souvenirs At the Night Bazaar And Then Eat At The Food Court

The Night Bazaar is a huge market that goes on nightly on the east side of Chiang Mai. It runs along Chang Klan Road between Tha Pae and Sridonchai Roads. This market is where you can find a wide array of goods, from handmade Thai goods to clothing and shoes to electronics to art. There are actually numerous smaller markets inside the larger umbrella market named the Night Bazaar if you wander off of the main street and into the covered areas. It is an excellent place to bargain, and you can often get items for half of the original asking price if you are persistent. While there are plenty of food stalls and restaurants sprinkled throughout the Night Bazaar, there is also an international food court, nestled behind the Pink Pvssy accessories shop on the northwest end of the Night Bazaar. The Ploen Ruedee Night Market is an atmospheric courtyard where you can enjoy tons of different foods, cocktails and beer, and live music most nights.

22. Don't Let The Bugs And Lizards Bother You

Many homes and businesses in Thailand are exposed to natural elements because of the tropical climate. Where there is exposure, there are also bugs and geckos. You will very likely see them everywhere you go, and it is a very normal part of everyday life in Chiang Mai. Some travelers have problems with the number of bugs and geckos they encounter, but it is inevitable. While you will see less of them in closed-door, air-conditioned restaurants than at outside venues, they still exist. The truth is that they are scared of you, too, and they are mostly harmless. Geckos end up in every room, whether it's a tightly sealed hotel room or an open-air space, and you will save a lot of energy by simply accepting their presence. If you tend to get bitten by mosquitoes, just wear repellent as normal. And if you don't want to find ants in your room, keep any and all food in a refrigerator.

23. Check Out The Many Vegetarian- and Vegan- Friendly Restaurants

Chiang Mai has a fabulous vegetarian and vegan community. There are quite a few restaurants around the city that are either largely or exclusively vegetarian or vegan, and in general, they come highly regarded. The vegan scene in Chiang Mai also seems to be growing, as I have noticed quite a few new exclusively vegan restaurants opening just in the past few months. Whether you are searching for Thai food, western comforts, brunch or snacks of the vegetarian or vegan variety, Chiang Mai has you covered! Some of the most-discussed restaurants around the city are Pun Pun, Amrita Garden, Bodhi Tree Cafe, Free Bird Cafe, and Alice's Organic. Wherever you are in the city, however, you'll likely be able to find vegetarian or vegan food near you with a quick internet search.

24. Know The Bathroom 411

Chiang Mai bathrooms are not one-in-the-same. This means that you cannot expect to find the same type of bathroom facilities everywhere you go. For example, on one visit you may be pleasantly surprised to find an electronic seat with a bidet and automatic seat cover. Another time you may find yourself in an outdoor bathroom with a squat toilet and a bucket of water—no flush, no tissue, no instructions. This was the case when I first arrived in Thailand, and I had no idea how to use a squat toilet. Needless to say, I found out afterward that I had done it all wrong. So it is highly recommended that you keep tissue with you during your travels—you will most likely need it at some point—and to read up on squat toilets before you come so that you know how to use them, just in case.

25. Try The Fresh Fruit

Thailand has some of the juiciest, tastiest fruits you'll ever try. As an American visiting Southeast Asia for the first time, I came to realize that fruit tastes so much better fresh from the source than purchased from a local supermarket. Pineapple never tasted so good, mangoes are abundant—try the mango sticky rice dessert—and fresh coconut water and flesh are a sweet, sweet way to stay hydrated in the heat. Try fresh fruit smoothies as well, to be found almost everywhere. Smoothies are a Thai staple since everyone loves to cool down from the heat with a fresh cold beverage. Don't be afraid to experiment with some of the unfamiliar fruits you might see while strolling through a market or ordering a smoothie. Dragonfruit, mangosteen, lychee, rambutan, and papaya are all delicious exotic treats that could introduce you to a new favorite fruit! You will not have to travel far to find fruit, either. It is offered at every market, from street vendors on many of the busier roads, in supermarkets, and at the majority of restaurants.

26. Watch A Muay Thai Fight, Or Take A Class!

Muay Thai, or Thai boxing, is a cherished sport in Thailand, and Chiang Mai has a few stadiums where you can check out a live fight and relish the exciting atmosphere. Normally they put on a show of sorts in between fights, where people get in the ring and make you laugh with their fake combat. If you don't like to sit on the sidelines, check out one of the many Muay Thai gyms around the city for a lesson or two! You'll be able to find highly trained Muay Thai professionals to teach you the basics and give you an intense workout.

27. Plan A Day Trip To Doi Inthanon

Doi Inthanon is Thailand's tallest mountain, and it happens to be only about an hour's drive from the city. It's a very popular destination for locals and visitors alike due to its size and the array of activities it has to offer. You can visit the very top of the mountain and feel a massive temperature shift while exploring the sacred ground, although you will have to wander a bit lower in order to find a viewpoint, as the very top of the mountain is surrounded by trees. You can also walk or rest alongside the several rushing waterfalls around the mountain, take a hike along the nature trails, gaze around at the beauty of the king and queen's pagodas and the surrounding, lush garden, and even camp overnight with a fabulous sunrise view. Day trips to Doi Inthanon are very popular and can be booked at any tourism office, or possibly at the front desk of your accommodation. My visit to Doi Inthanon is one of my most memorable experiences from my first week in Chiang Mai, and especially the pagodas.

28. Eat Thai Curry

If you have not yet tried Thai curry, you should while you are in town. Thai curries use more fresh herbs than dried spices, like other curries, and their coconut milk component gives them a soup consistency. There are five varieties of Thai curry, and they are all worth a try. Choose from green, yellow, red, panang, and masaman. They all have similar basic ingredients, yet the chilis and extra ingredients added give each curry a unique flavor. So whether or not you have enjoyed other curries from other countries, Thai curries are quite unique and there is bound to be one that agrees with your taste buds.

29. Grab Dinner At One Of The Nightly Food Markets

Some of the most popular dining spots for locals are the markets that pop up after 5:00 pm around town. Some of the biggest ones are located at Chang Phuak Gate on the north end of the old city, as well as the opposite end, at Chiang Mai gate. The go-to food stop for students is the nightly market right outside the back gate of Chiang Mai University on Suthep Road. Whichever market you find yourself at, it's fun to do a full lap and see all of the interesting choices before you decide what to have. If you're with a group, a smorgasbord is always a fun option so that you can taste more foods in one sitting. It might also be a good idea to scout out the busier food stalls and find out what the locals are eating!

30. Visit The Grand Canyon And Its New Water Park

The Grand Canyon is a man-made reservoir located less than 30 minutes from the old city by motorbike or car. Those who visit enjoy swimming in the reservoir and lounging in the shade while surrounded by scenic cliffs. The Canyon has been growing in popularity over the past few years, and as such it has gone through updates that include the creation of a brand new water park with slides and an inflatable floating ropes course. The location also hosts events, such as the Jai Thep Festival taking place in February. There is also an on-site cafe offering food, beverages, and souvenirs.

31. Get Soaked During Songkran

Songkran is the Thai new year, which takes place during burning season in mid-April. This is the biggest holiday in Thailand's calendar year, and most of the country has time off to celebrate. Thai people traditionally begin the new year by making merit, paying reverence to ancestors and pouring water on both Buddha statues and other people as a symbol of purification. While Songkran takes place during the hottest, smoggiest time of year, the unique festivities associated with Songkran often keep revelers from overheating. With the holiday comes the water festival, during which water is thrown from trucks, squirted from guns, poured from balconies and splashed from buckets while celebrators clad bright festive clothing and walk around with their valuables wrapped in plastic. There are ceremonies, parades, and parties all around Chiang Mai, and the positive energy is palpable all around the country.

32. Watch A Cabaret Show

The ladyboy cabaret shows are nightly events taking place in the Night Bazaar district of Chiang Mai. These shows are highly entertaining, with extravagant costumes, grand performances, and good humor as the main attractions of the evening. It is easy to tell, when watching, that the performers put in a lot of hard work to make their shows the best they can be. They are playful and love to flirt with audience members as they make their way through the crowds during their songs. They allow you to take pictures with them after the show if you're willing to tip them. The most popular cabaret show is in the Anusarn Market within the Night Bazaar. Tickets for this show tend to sell quickly, so arrive early to purchase yours in order to get a good seat! You can also check out Ram Bar's cabaret show, also in the Night Bazaar area, where the vicinity is smaller, but the performances are arguably bigger.

33. Travel On A Budget With Ease

It's true that all of Thailand provides travelers with a bargain holiday. But Chiang Mai is especially inexpensive. Modern accommodation with air-conditioning can be as cheap as 300 baht per night. Street food generally costs between 30 and 60 baht for a meal. Day trips with food and transportation included can be as low as 1000 baht. Motorbikes can be rented for 200 baht per day and massages start at the same price. And, because of the low cost of living, those who are not necessarily on a budget are also in for a treat. High quality is available for significantly less than you will find elsewhere, so travelers wanting elegance can easily find accommodation and restaurants to their standards at bargain prices.

34. Eat At Cherng Doi Chicken

This restaurant is frequented by locals and has also become a popular lunch and dinner spot for visitors. Cherng Doi has great grilled chicken, as the name suggests, as well as a myriad of other foods out of the Isaan region of Thailand. Try one of the warm salads like nam tok or laab (warm meat salads), or bamboo salad. You will also want to order classic som tum (papaya salad) or one of their som tum varieties. The fried som tum is a tasty, unique choice if you're really hungry! Drinks such as iced tea and beer are also available. The restaurant has menus with pictures to help make the ordering process easy, and normally the food comes out quickly.

35. Take A Trip To Mon Cham

On a hill ridge overlooking valleys on either side, is Mon Cham. This picturesque location is located north of Chiang Mai and into the mountains of Mae Rim. Here you can savor the crisp mountain air, drink coffee, enjoy a meal, and gaze at the unbelievable views. You can also choose to stay overnight in a tent or a bungalow and wake up to see the sun rising over the mountain. It's a sight you won't regret staying for. And on your way up, or down the mountain, stop at one of the produce stands at the foot of the mountain and treat yourself to fresh strawberries or fruit wine made right on the mountain.

36. Rent Motorbikes And Ride The Samoeng Loop

Adventurers who feel confident riding a motorbike should consider this road trip. The Samoeng Loop is a scenic drive around the outskirts and into the mountains of Chiang Mai. It's a unique way to see the province, with fresh air and endless lush greenery all around you. This approximate 100-kilometer loop can be done within a day—about 4-5 hours if you make stops along the way. The drive will take you through Samoeng town, Mae Sa Valley with beautiful vista views and waterfalls, and Mae Rim. You can choose to do the loop clockwise or anti-clockwise, and maps can be printed or picked up for free at local bike rental shops.

37. Eat Chiang Mai Food At Tong Tem Toh

If you are looking to try authentic Northern Thai food, Tong Tem Toh will not disappoint. Located on Soi 13 in the Nimman area of the city, Tong Tem Toh serves a huge menu of unique northern dishes to try. It's a fabulous place to share plates in order to try many different foods in one sitting. This restaurant is well-loved by locals and visitors alike, and it gets crowded every evening. In order to avoid a wait, you will want to arrive around 5:00 pm. Some must-try items are the grilled pork shoulder, steamed chicken in banana leaf, and the beef soup.

38. Visit the Hidden Terracotta Art Garden

Tucked behind a tall brick wall on the south end of the old city is Ban Phor Liang Meun's Terracotta Arts Garden. The garden isn't really hidden, but it is easy to pass by without noticing. It can certainly make visitors feel as though they have stepped out of Chiang Mai and into a different realm. Upon entering, you find yourself in a serene garden where the air is cool and quiet. Terracotta artwork in varying sizes and styles fill the space. Find clay sculpture plaques, lanterns, wall panels, statues and more as you stroll along the stone pathway. There is scattered seating for those who wish to sit and admire the fresh air and the beautiful fusion of art and nature. Prolong your stay with a drink or a meal at the Coffee by Clay Studio, a glass-enclosed, on-site cafe with views of the enchanted garden.

39. Get Breakfast At Baan Bakery

Thailand is not a big bread-consuming country, but expats and travelers find an oasis in bakeries like Baan Bakery. Located just south of the old city, this place serves up the most delicious, fresh baked goods—croissants, danishes, loaves of bread—and they also make delectable hot sandwiches and good coffee. Baan Bakery opens at 8:00 am and does not close until 4:00 pm, but because of high demand, they often sell out of most of their pastries near lunch time. So if you are hoping to try a danish or a croissant, be sure to arrive early! They offer their high-quality bakery at very reasonable prices, and they always serve you with a smile.

40. Relax In A Bamboo Hut At Huay Tung Tao

Huay Tung Tao, just 20 minutes north of the city, is a large lake overlooking the mountains of Doi Pui. All around the lake are restaurants offering bamboo huts for you to relax in while enjoying classic Thai food and a beverage or two. A road runs around the entire lake, so you are also welcome to walk, run or bike there. It is a common place for Thai people to spend an afternoon eating, drinking, talking and relaxing. If you are in search of a tranquil way to spend part of your day, enjoy the serenity and the proximity of the Doi Pui landscape while unwinding like a local!

41. Become Informed About Thai Animal Welfare Issues

There has been a lot of news circulating recently regarding issues of wild animals used for profit and entertainment in Thailand. They are often treated poorly, drugged or otherwise subdued, and harmed behind the scenes of animal parks across the country, and Chiang Mai is no exception. It would be against Thai law to name specific locations that you would do well to avoid. Just please research reviews of any companies that offer animal entertainment with elephants, monkeys, or tigers before you commit. There are alternatives that will still allow you to get up close to an animal without supporting unethical practices.

42. Eat And Shop Organic At Pun Pun Market

Pun Pun is an organic farm and sustainable learning center in Chiang Mai. They serve their vegetables at their two restaurants, and they offer natural food and health products in their shop at the market location near Airport Plaza right off of Hang Dong Road. Fill up on their fresh fusion wraps, Thai food, and smoothies in the restaurant. Then browse the adjacent store for fresh kombucha, snacks, herbs and homemade soaps among other goods. It's a peaceful location where you can gaze at staff tending to their garden while enjoying the open air seating without city noise.

43. Find A Good Place To See A Sunset

The sunsets each evening over Doi Suthep and it's quite a sight to see. No matter how long a person spends in Chiang Mai, each dusk feels no less magical as the last one when the sunset is within view. There are a number of rooftop bars throughout the city, such as the top of Maya shopping center, Rise Rooftop Bar, The Roof at Sala Lana Hotel, and Hotel YaYee. Or, for a more natural atmosphere, head over to the Ang Kaew Reservoir on the beautiful Chiang Mai University Campus and get a front-row seat!

44. Eat Other International Foods, Not Only Thai

Chiang Mai is a haven for expats, and luckily this makes Chiang Mai a hub of international foods as well. Whatever you fancy, Chiang Mai is likely to offer it! You can find great sushi, Korean fried chicken, pizza, Indian food, burgers, Mexican dishes, breakfasts and brunches with a simple search. Prices can range widely, and you will certainly have luck finding great cuisine for reasonable prices. So if you have been dining Thai and you're craving something else, you won't be disappointed.

45. Check The Current Events While You're Here

Thailand never misses an opportunity to celebrate, and pop-up markets and events happen all the time in Chiang Mai. Quite often they center around food, as food is at the center of culture and conversation in Thailand. Inquire with the staff at your accommodation or online to find out if anything special is happening in the city during your visit. Or, if you happen across an event while exploring the city, check it out! If you do, you will find a perfect opportunity to hear Thai entertainment, eat new Thai foods, and browse the booths of handmade art and goods that might not be found at any of the regular markets.

46. Celebrate Loi Krathong

Loi Krathong is an annual Thai festival that takes place on the evening of the full moon in November. Krathongs are baskets made of buoyant banana trunks—or styrofoam or bread— which are then decorated, filled with candles, incense, and sometimes money, and then traditionally they are released onto a river. The sentiment behind Loi Krathong is to release bad luck, ask forgiveness for wrongdoing, pray for good fortune and set intentions for the year. The highly publicized lantern component of Loi Krathong is less conventional, but it comes with the same sentiment. Lanterns are released with the hopes and intentions of people across Chiang Mai. The river and the night sky light up over the course of the night, creating a magical atmosphere of new beginnings and positive intentions.

47. Get A Massage

As you wander around Chiang Mai, you will notice that massages are offered around every corner. Not only that, but they are also inexpensive. At small shops situated around the city, prices normally range between 200 and 500 baht for your choice of massage. At the more renowned spas across Chiang Mai, prices and levels of service rise. You can ask for a Thai massage if your muscles require intense loosening, but most locations also offer regular back and shoulder massages with or without oil, and foot reflexology. Massages are also offered at the weekend markets for lower prices, so look out for them. Wherever you decide to go, you will be doing yourself a favor by taking advantage of the availability and affordability of massages in Chiang Mai.

48. Use Activated Charcoal & Colloidal Silver To Stay Healthy

The food is delicious, but inevitably we hear stories about travelers, and even long-term expats for that matter, developing acute stomach issues while in Chiang Mai. You can never guess where or when it will happen, or which meals will adversely affect which people, but you can be prepared. As a precaution before a meal, or afterward, if you begin to feel symptoms, take an activated charcoal tablet or a dose of colloidal silver water. Both remedies are widely approved ways of making sure you stay healthy while tasting your way through Chiang Mai! You don't have to bring them from home, either. You can find charcoal tablets at one of the countless pharmacies around the city. Colloidal silver can be found at some of the local health food stores and restaurants like Aden, Urban Green, and Food 4 Thought.

49. Go On A Mountain Biking Tour

Chiang Mai and all of Northern Thailand is a biking oasis of mountains and lavish landscapes. Cycling is a highly popular activity for people living and traveling in the area. You can choose to borrow a bicycle on your own from one of the many shops renting them by the day, or you can go on a group tour. If you haven't biked much before, leisurely scenic tours are offered around the outskirts of the city that you can choose from. And more advanced riders can browse a long list of route types and distances ranging from half a day to two full days of riding. Mountain Biking Chiang Mai is a good place to begin your biking journey!

50. Let Your Feet Hang While You Eat At Huai Kha

For an atmospheric, unique dining experience, this restaurant does not disappoint. Huai Kha, located near the southwest corner of the old city, is a Thai food restaurant where guests remove their shoes before climbing the stairs to the second floor, classic wooden open-air restaurant and sit on cushions around a lowered table. Your feet dangle in the air, as the floor beneath the table has been removed. The restaurant has dim lighting and a pleasant ambiance, and the staff is very attentive. They also have an extensive menu of great quality, and you'll see many locals dining around you. If you want to enjoy quality Thai food in a charming restaurant, look no further.

\>TOURIST

BRZENK

> TOURIST
GREATER THAN A TOURIST

Visit GreaterThanATourist.com:

http://GreaterThanATourist.com

Sign up for the Greater Than a Tourist Newsletter:

http://eepurl.com/cxspyf

Follow us on Facebook:

https://www.facebook.com/GreaterThanATourist

Follow us on Pinterest:

http://pinterest.com/GreaterThanATourist

Follow us on Instagram:

http://Instagram.com/GreaterThanATourist

BRZENK

> TOURIST
GREATER THAN A TOURIST

Please leave your honest review of this book on Amazon and Goodreads. Thank you. We appreciate your positive and constructive feedback. Thank you.

NOTES

Made in the USA
Middletown, DE
15 September 2023

38569634R00050